Ancient Greece

A Captivating Guide to Greek History Starting from the Greek Dark Ages to the End of Antiquity

Free Bonus from Captivating History (Available for a Limited time)

Hi History Lovers!

Now you have a chance to join our exclusive history list so you can get your first history ebook for free as well as discounts and a potential to get more history books for free! Simply visit the link below to join.

Captivatinghistory.com/ebook

Also, make sure to follow us on:

Twitter: @Captivhistory

Facebook: CaptivatingHistory:@captivatinghistory

Contents

Introduction

The period commonly referred to as Ancient Greece spans a broad scope of time from the Grecian Dark Ages in approximately 1100 BC to the End of Antiquity in around AD 600. Just as the time is extensive in range, so was the geography of Greece. Over that period, in fact, the borders sometimes grew to encompass many other modern-day regions. At other times, the boundaries shrank, and for a period the region was under the dominion of the Roman Empire. Even still, the reach of Greece was strong, with neighbouring areas being profoundly influenced by Greek culture and events.

The culture and events of Greece were so influential they have a significant effect on modern-day people all over the world. The ancient Greeks gave birth to democracy, a political system frequently used and considered by some as the best form of government. Great minds from Greece also made incredible and vital discoveries such as the water mill, the basics of geometry and using medicine to cure illness. The ancient Greek philosophers laid the groundwork for a whole new field of thought and study. Ancient Greece offered the foundation of the Olympic games, which still run regularly today. Particularly famous historical figures such as Alexander the Great and Cleopatra also had ties to and roles during Greek history, through the course of wars and empire expansion.

Given the influence of Ancient Greece, as you learn about this time and place, you will learn about your history and the origins of the people, places, and institutions you likely regularly studied in school. Starting in the Dark Ages, it is quite a journey through the darkness, democracy, discovery, and development of Western Civilization.

Chapter 1 – Dawn of the Dark Ages

For approximately 500 years, the Mycenaean civilization resided in the geographic area now known as Greece. In about 1200 BC, the Mycenaean civilization started to collapse. Archaeological records suggest that by around 1100 BC, the cities, outlying settlements, and the entire organization of the Mycenaeans' culture began to be abandoned or destroyed. By 1050 BC, the recognizable features of Mycenaean culture had nearly entirely disappeared, and the population was significantly reduced. Many historians provide explanations for the cause of this downturn. Some attribute the fall of the Mycenaean civilization, which coincided with the collapse the Bronze Age, to climatic or environmental catastrophe. Others attribute it to invasion by the Dorians or the "Sea Peoples." No single explanation fits all the available archaeological evidence.

Invasions by a group known as the "Sea Peoples" may have contributed to the collapse of the Mycenaean civilization. Their exact origins remain a mystery. The "Sea Peoples" may have come from as far away as the northern shores of the Black Sea, or from as close nearby as the Aegean Sea or from along the Mediterranean coasts of Asia Minor. The Egyptians named these peoples, in inscriptions and carvings at Karnak and Luxor. The Egyptians had some initial military successes against these foreign warriors. However, even Egypt could not escape the repercussions of these attacks, which spanned the entirety of the Eastern Mediterranean, subsuming the area of modern-day Greece, and leading to the dawn of the Dark Ages.

The collapse of Mycenaean civilization caused significant disruptions to people's way of life in the region. There was economic hardship, famine, and political instability. Large-scale revolts took place, and powerful kingdoms were wholly overthrown. Crucial trade connections were lost. Towns and villages were abandoned or burned to the ground. The population of Greece was reduced, perhaps by half, and whole systems of organization ceased: state armies, kings, administrators, and trade connections disappeared.

Due to the collapse of large cities, great planned construction projects and wall painting for the arts could not continue to completion. The use of the Linear B writing system ceased. This reduced the ability for record keeping and therefore information on this period in Greek history comes only from the remains and artifacts found in burial sites.

The fragmented societies that remained were mostly isolated from one another, and thus each developed their own cultures, pottery styles, burial practices, and other settlement features. Again, records are almost non-existent, but pottery has been found in archaeological sites. The pottery style, which is known as Proto-Geometric, was substantially less complex than designs that existed before the collapse. This is a sign that progress in development had been lost and in some cases, even regressed.

It is likely that during this period, the divisions of the region were organized by kinship groups and the oikoi (or households). This style laid the origins of the later poleis (political nature of Greece). Due to the disparate societies, generalizations about a more extensive community cannot be made. The various people throughout the region that survived the initial collapse cannot be grouped in any meaningful way because they spent too much time disconnected from each other. Some areas in Greece, such as Attica, Euboea, and central Crete, recovered their economy faster than others.

Luckily, not all was lost for the future of the region. There were still some advances during this time. They were just limited and slower in progress than they may have otherwise been. There was still farming, weaving, metalworking, and pottery, but at a much lower level of output and only for local consumption. There was some limited technical progress, such as a faster potter's wheel and the developm-ent of the compass (for the drawing of geometric patterns). Longer lasting glazes were also developed by higher firing temperature.

Perhaps most importantly and influential for the ongoing history of the region, methods for smelting iron came from Cyprus and the Levant, and drew upon local sources of iron ore. Iron weapons were now within reach of less elite warriors, and the universal adoption of iron was a critical feature for most Dark Age settlements. From 1050 onward, several local iron industries appeared, and by 900, almost all graves contained at least some iron implements.

With time and work, some communities were able to return from their setbacks. Archaeologists can study these communities to better understand their structure and the timing of events. For example, excavations of Dark Age communities such as Nicosia in the Peloponnese have demonstrated how a Bronze Age town was abandoned in 1150 but then re-emerged as a small cluster of villages by 1075.

At that time, only around 40 families were living there with plenty of good farming land and grazing for cattle. The remains of a 10th-century building, including a megaron (great hall typical of Greek palaces), on the top of the ridge, have led to speculation this was the leader's house or a place of religious significance. This was a larger structure than those surrounding it, but it was still made from the same materials (mud brick and thatched roof).

High-status individuals did, in fact, exist in the Dark Ages, but their standard of living was not significantly higher than others in their village. Most Greeks did not live in isolated farmsteads because living far from organized societies increased the danger and risk of being attacked by enemies. Instead, they lived in small settlements. It is likely that for the next two to three hundred years, the primary economic source for most families was through farming on their ancestral plot of land.

The archaeological records show that by the start of the 8th century BC, several sites in Greece saw robust economic recovery. Long distance trade was re-established, by connecting the Near East, Greece, Egypt, and Italy. Archaeological findings show Greek pottery in northern Syria and among the Villanovan culture in Italy, which shows evidence for those trade routes.

As time passed, the forms, styles, and decoration of pottery became more complex and included figurative scenes that appear to come from the Homeric Epics *The Iliad* and *The Odyssey*. This showed that attention to the arts had re-emerged. Iron tools and weapons also continued to develop and increased in quality.

Mediterranean trade brought new supplies of copper and tin to the region of Greece from distant places. This allowed artisans to craft a wide variety of elaborate bronze tools and items. Other coastal regions of Greece were once again becoming full participants in the commercial and cultural exchanges of the eastern and central Mediterranean. Simultaneously, local governance increased in complexity, changing from single-leader autocracies to oligarchies or other forms of aristocratic rulership.

Although the region of Greece had faced its Dark Ages, which brought setbacks to their way of life. The people re-built all that was lost. As methods for government started to evolve there, the region moved from the Dark ages into the enlightenment of Democracy.

Chapter 2 – From Darkness to Democracy

As the region of Greece moved away from the demand for mere survival brought about by the Dark Ages, the people could think about living well. The existing state organization, government, and political leadership had been comprised of many separate, but equal groups. Luckily, the Grecian people saw a better solution than just infighting for power. They envisioned a solution for governance that would allow all people to be considered equally. It was a revolutionary approach, and one many countries use today— Democracy.

The development of Democracy among the Greek city-states was slow, yet continually developing process. Democracy in Athens grew in fits and starts, but eventually, it blossomed to its fullest extent. Its humble beginnings began with the politician Solon.

In the period before Solon's leadership, most of the city-states had tyrannical (rule by a single person), aristocratic, or oligarchic governments. Then, in 632 BC, following the misinterpreted advice of an oracle, a nobleman named Cylon, attempted a coup in Athens. The coup failed with Cylon, his brother, and other followers seeking refuge in the Temple of Athena. Cylon and his brother eventually escaped. The attempted coup resulted in a period of shifting alliances and economic stagnation in Athens.

In approximately 593 BC, due to the political climate of the time, Solon was given almost unlimited power when he was elected to the office of Archon. Solon decided to write dictates designed to solve the political problems plaguing the city. Solon's dictates were inscribed on wooden plaques that were hung up for the citizens to read. Solon repealed all the laws (except those concerning homicide).

Before Solon's reforms, Athens was administered by nine Archons, who were elected or appointed. There was also an assembly of commoners (the *ekklesia*). However, there was no representative body for the lowest class of citizens (the Thetes). Solon altered the rules for the *ekklesia*, allowing all male citizens to be allowed into it, with court magistrates and juries drawn from the same pool of males. This could be considered as an early version of the Republic form of government, in which citizens have a role in the creation of laws and the means to hold elected leaders accountable.

To guide such a large governing body, Solon also created the Council of Four Hundred. For this, each of the four Athenian tribes put forward one hundred members to serve on the Council. Solon also made alterations to the organization of Athens' military by stratifying the roles and delineating who could serve in them according to their family wealth or property.

Solon also reformed the economic laws and culture of Athens. Fathers were encouraged to find trades or suitable economic roles for their sons. Otherwise, the sons would not be required to support their fathers in old age. Foreign craftsmen and merchants were encouraged to move to Athens with their families and were granted citizenship. The cultivation of olives and the production of olive-based products was supported, and the export of all other produce was prohibited. Solon also propagated laws regarding some forms of slavery: annulling all contracts based on personal servitude, banning debt-based slavery, and releasing all Athenian citizens from all forms of slavery. Furthermore, Solon also passed several other social reforms to improve Athenian life.

Once his rules were disseminated, and he saw they were working, Solon left Athens for ten years, travelling the various territories of the Eastern Mediterranean. The reforms did not last long, however, as the old ways were challenging to give up. Within four years, some elected officials refused to stand down once their terms were up, while other important posts sometimes remained empty. Eventually, a relative of Solon, Peisistratus, seized power as a tyrant ruling over Athens. Upon returning after his ten years, Solon regarded the Athenians as foolish for allowing this to happen.

After Peisistratus died in 527 BC, his son, Hippias, became a tyrant. Hippias was cruel to the citizens of Athens. He levied crushing taxes on the poor and executed large numbers of people. This caused immense hostility towards his rule, and he began looking abroad for allies, first in Persia and then in Lampsakos. Other Athenian families, concerned about any relationship with Persia, sought to overthrow Hippias. Eventually, he was ousted by a Spartan military campaign in 510 BC and banished from Athens along with his family. Hippias and his family joined the Achaemenid Empire.

Following the expulsion of Hippias, democracy was brought back through the reforms of Cleisthenes, during 508 BC. His first change altered the political boundaries of Athens, broadening them to contain the entire region of Attica, and regarding all the free people there as citizens. Further changes were made in 462 BC by Ephialtes, which significantly reduced the power of the existing leadership body, turning it solely into a court for the trying of deliberate homicide. In the fourth century BC, the leadership body was again modified, adding responsibility for investigating corruption among officials.

By the fourth century BC, Athenian democracy had reached its maturity. Like today, some Athenians were more politically active or ambitious than others. The governing bodies of the city were complex, multi-faceted, and involved a 'checks-and-balances' system to ensure stability. To vote, one had to be an adult, male citizen. Aside from participation in politics, being male certainly gave ancient Grecians many more rights and abilities. Something that was also demonstrated in the ancient Olympic games.

Chapter 3 – Olympic Origins

In addition to benefiting from the wisdom of Greek democracy, Ancient Greece also offered a gift to future generations through the Olympic games.

Some historians believe the Olympics date back to 10th or 9th century BC. However, it is most likely the first Olympic games took place in 776 BC in Olympia (named for Mt. Olympus, the home of the Greek Gods and Goddesses). It is unclear who invented the games. Mythology says Zeus, who was the father of the other Greek Gods and Goddesses, instituted the games to commemorate his battle with Kronos. Some attribute the founding to Heracles (Hercules, a demi-God).

At the time, the Olympic games were part of a religious festival intended to honour Zeus. They were also a time for a truce and good relations between the Greek cities. Men from all over Greece (including Spain and Turkey, which were subsumed under Greece at that time) would arrive at that Sanctuary of Zeus in Olympia, to represent their city-states by showing their physical prowess and skill. They would enter through the Portico of Echo and perform in an ancient stadium.

During the first Olympic games, there may have been only one significant event—a stadium race around a 600-foot-long track. During the first Olympic showing, a cook from Elis, named Koroibos, won that contest. Records indicate this singular athletic event may have constituted the Olympic games for the next 13 Olympic festivals (until 724 BC, with the Olympics happening only every four years). In contrast to today's medals, during the ancient Olympic games, winners were recognized with olive wreaths.

Starting in 720 BC, the games expanded by adding other events. Some also believe in that year the practice of nudity during the games became common. However, it is not clear when this tradition started, who instituted it, or why it was done. It is most likely it did become standard practice by the late 8th century BC. Early on, all Olympic events were held on just one day, but as events were added, they extended it to five days.

When events were added, running was divided into three events: the stage (a test of speed ran the length of the stadium), the diaulos (two lengths of the stadium), and the dolichos (20 lengths of the stadium). Wrestling was used to represent military combat without weapons. Boxers hands were protected with leather. Some combatants even added metal to the hand joints, to make the punches more painful. Pankration was an ancient form of martial arts that combined elements of wrestling and boxing. The equestrian competitions were played in the Hippodrome, rather than the stadium and the winner was the owner of the horse, not the rider himself. The pentathlon was comprised of five events: wrestling, javelin, long jump, running, and discuss. There were also boys' events, including boxing, wrestling, and running.

Some of the best champions from the Olympics were heralded in historical records. Often statues were made in their likeness and placed in their hometowns. There was Astylos of Kroton, who won six olive wreaths over the course of multiple Olympics. His victories were met with some challenges. In his first games, he represented Kroton. Later, he represented Syracuse, and the Krotons punished him by destroying his statue.

Milon, also from Kroton, had brains and brawn. He studied under Pythagoras (ancient Greek geometrician). He won six times for wrestling, at the Olympics. He also won seven times in the Pythian Games, ten times in the Isthmian Games, and nine times in the Nemean Games. He was certainly one of Greece's most celebrated athletes.

Leonidas of Rhodes also won numerous victories. He, in fact, won three separate events at four consecutive Olympics. Melankomas of Karia was celebrated for his talents in boxing. He was light and quick, usually defeating an opponent without being hit or hitting them. He would fight by holding his arms out and dodging their blows until they became too exhausted to fight.

Although women were not permitted to participate in the ancient Olympics, Kyniska of Sparta (daughter of King Archidamus), still found a way to win. She was the first woman to be listed as an Olympic victor when her chariot won in races during the 96th and 97th Olympics. At the time, victories were awarded to the owner of the chariot and horse, not the actual rider. Sadly, her stealthy victory took recognition from the rider.

Although many associate marathon running with the ancient Olympics, the first marathon did not occur during Ancient times. This practice was instituted during the modern Olympics. It was done to commemorate the run of Pheidippides, who carried news from Marathon to Athens (approximately 26 miles) during 490 BC. An event that is entirely separate from the Olympic games.

Later still, after conquering Greece, the Romans also joined the Olympic games. The ancient Olympic games occurred until AD 393. It is believed Emperor Theodosius I, decided the games were representative of pagan cults, and he had them abolished. Olympia was then attacked by vandalism. Earthquakes and floods also damaged it. The area eventually disappeared. It was rediscovered in 1766 by Englishman Richard Chandler. However, it was only in 1875 that archaeological digs found Olympic ruins.

It was not until 1503 years after the final ancient Olympic game that the games returned in 1896. A Frenchman, Baron Pierre de Coubertin initiated the idea of holding modern Olympic games. Although he initially wanted the games to be held in Paris, after some planning and organizing, it was decided the first modern Olympics would be held in Athens, Greece. The Olympics now occur every two years, alternating between Summer and Winter games, and in different locations around the world.

One central tradition of the modern Olympics is the passing of the Olympic torch and the lighting of the Olympic flame. This idea of an Olympic flame was first used in 1928 during the Amsterdam games. The first torch relay occurred in the 1936 Berlin games. Torch relays were not explicitly used in the ancient Olympic games. However, they were often used in other Greek athletic festivals, including some held in Athens.

Although the ancient Olympic games were a time of truce when people came together to show their athletic skill. There were still tensions among people as cities and states used the opportunity to prove the superiority of their region. Moreover, those truces were confined to the period of each game, and there were still plenty of wars occurring in the years between games that continued to reshape Greece and grow its history forward.

Chapter 4 – Greece Grows from War to War

Even while the Olympics were occurring every four years, conflict brewed among the Greeks. The primary conflict was the Messenian wars of which there were three. It is not entirely clear when the first occurred because three historians give separate and differing accounts. They each use a different measure or calendar system. Most modern historians believe the first Messenian War likely started in 757 BC.

The precipitating events for the first Messenian War date back to approximately 400 years before. Sometime around the year 1100 BC, the Heracleidae returned to the Peloponnesus to reclaim their birth right. The Heracleidae are supposedly the direct descendants of Hercules and are, ethnically and linguistically, Dorian Greeks. These peoples conquered or supplanted the leadership of various cities and regions within the Peloponnesus. This resulted in changes to the ethnic mix of the entire Greek mainland.

Doric groups spread throughout the southern two-thirds of the Peloponnesus and the cities of Epirus; Achaeans occupied the northern portions of the Peloponnesus; Ionians occupied Attica, southern Thrace and Macedonia, various Aegean Islands, and the lands that would eventually become Ionia in Asia Minor; and Aeolians occupied Thebes and the cities of Thessaly. Conflict arose sporadically between the rulers of these cities and regions, mainly since many of the citizens were not of the same ethnic group as the rulers. These divisions. both internally and externally continued to impact Greece all the way through to the Peloponnesian War.

A distal cause of the First Messenian War involved the lineage and culture of the Kings of Messenia. The Messenians, most of whom were Achaean, were initially accepting of their new Dorian overlord,

Cresphontes after he married Merope (the daughter of King Cypselus of Arcadia, who was Achaean). At some point, Cresphontes and Merope surrendered some land to a group of Dorians, forming a Dorian enclave within Messenia.

The subjects of Messenia revolted, killing Cresphontes and all but one of his children, Aepytus, who was being educated in Arcadia at the time. Once Aepytus reached adulthood, he was installed as King of Messenia by the various other Dorian monarchs in the Peloponnesus. This would later backfire on them, however, as Aepytus began a program of systematically wiping out the Dorian culture in Messenia and replacing it with his adopted Achaean culture. This enraged the Dorian subjects within Messenia and the Dorian kings who installed him to his throne.

The most proximate cause of the First Messenian War was a case of cattle rustling. Polychares of Messenia, who was an Olympic athlete, leased some grazing land from Euaiphnos of Spartan. Euaiphnos then stole the cattle and sold them, claiming raiders had ambushed the land and taken them. Polychares initially believed the explanation, but a herdsman of Polychares returned and explained what Euaiphnos had done.

Polychares was willing to let the cattle go, but Euaiphnos offered to take Polychares' son with him to pick up the money from the merchants. However, once out of Messenia, Euaiphnos killed Polychares' son. Polychares requested justice from Spartan magistrates. Justice was delayed, so Polychares decided to begin killing every Spartan he could find. After several murders, the Spartans demanded the extradition of Polychares to Sparta to stand trial. Rulers in Messenia were willing but wanted Euaiphnos in exchange.

By now, a simple case of the theft and sale of cattle had grown to involve the kings of Sparta and Messenia. Sparta dispatched a group of magistrates to Messenia to argue for the extradition of Polychares. At that time, two men ruled Messenia: Antiochus and Androcles (both were direct descendants of Aepytus). Androcles supported extraditing Polychares, while Antiochus was against it entirely.

At some point, the arguments between the rulers and the Spartan delegation boiled over, and both sides drew weapons. At the end of the fight, Androcles lay dead. Antiochus managed to calm the situation, wishing to turn the argument over to neutral arbitration (courts at Argos and Athens). None of that would happen, as Antiochus would be dead within three months, with his son Euphues succeeding him as sole King of Messenia. Shortly after his ascension, Sparta launched an invasion of Messenia.

For the first four years of the war, there was no progress by either side. In the fifth year, there was a tremendous battle near Ampheia. It was concluded indecisively, but with substantial losses on both sides. Not wanting to face such losses in the future, the Messenians fell back to a fortress at Mount Ithome. Around this time, a devastating plague struck Messenia, killing thousands of people. Distressed by mounting battlefield losses and losses at home to the plague, King Euphues sent a messenger to the Oracle at Delphi seeking advice on how to confront the Spartan threat. The Oracle instructed him to sacrifice a royal virgin, which they did. The Spartans, hearing of the Oracle's advice and the actions of the Messenians, withdrew for six years.

The war continued to wage on for years. This was a time where wars were fought in small segments between seasons and farm work. It severely restricted the time in which wars could be fought. This caused wars to last years or decades; even if the fighting could have been otherwise condensed and concluded within a few years. Though during the Messenian wars, the Greeks did advance their techniques with hoplites (career military soldiers), which made later combats more efficient.

In the 18th year of the war, several other Greek cities joined the conflict: Corinth joined with Sparta, while Arcadia and Sikyon joined with Messenia. For a short time, the tide turned in favour of the Messenians with the defeat of the Laconians, who had sided with Sparta. At some point, King Aristodemos of Messenia had a dream in which his daughter (who had been sacrificed at the suggestion of the Oracle of Delphi, appeared, and showed him her wounds). He awoke, went to her tomb, and killed himself. In the chaos that followed, the Messenians abandoned Mount Ithome, and the Spartans burned it to the ground. At this victory, the Spartans subjugated all of Messenia, reducing the remaining population to the status of helots (enslaved people), and with that, the war was over.

The Second and Third Messenian Wars each had their roots in the ashes of the first war: helot discontent. Both were widespread helot rebellions, first in 685 BC and then again in 464 BC. The first rebellion was concentrated within Messenia, where the local helots overthrew their overlords and, with the support of Argos, invaded Laconia. The initial invasion was successful, with the Messenians defeating the Spartans at the Battle of Deres. The Messenian leader of the battle, Aristomenes, was elevated by his soldiers into a king-like figure for Messenia; sharing lineage with Aepytus further cemented this.

Feeling particularly brave, or fool-hardy, Aristomenes snuck into Sparta and placed a shattered Spartan shield in the Temple of Athena to frighten the Spartans. It worked. The Spartans immediately sent for the wisdom of the Oracle at Delphi, who told them something they did not want to hear—they would need a leader from Athens to lead their armies to victory. The Spartans eventually, after suffering other battlefield losses, swallowed their collective pride to request help from Athens.

Athens sent them Tyrtaeus, who was lame (missing a leg), nearly blind, and a poet, not a military commander. Apparently, his poetry was uncommonly good, as after joining the Spartan army, the war turned in Sparta's favour, eventually trapping the Messenians in a fortress at Mount Ira. During a raid on a Spartan supply line, Aristomenes was captured.

Using the swiftness and guile that allowed him to sneak into Sparta, Aristomenes was able to slip his bonds and escape the Spartans before he could be executed, making it back to Mount Ira. The Messenians held off the Spartans for nearly a decade before surrendering. The Spartans allowed the women, children, and even Aristomenes to leave, telling those who stayed they would either die or be reduced to helot status again. Many left for Italy, settling a city at Messina. This was the end of the second war.

The Third Messenian War was a broader conflict, involving several different peoples who were subjugated as helots by Sparta. The war started in response to a devastating earthquake that struck Sparta in 464 BC. Modern analysis of the area suggests the quake had a surface wave magnitude of 7.6, which made it one of the strongest recorded earthquakes in all of antiquity. Scholars of the period put the immediate death toll between 10 and 20 thousand people. In its aftermath, the Laconians, Messenians, Thourians, and Aithaians all rebelled against Sparta. The revolt was so great the leaders of Sparta asked the other Greek city-states for assistance.

Most cities, including Athens, sent military delegations. However, Sparta concerned the Athenians had ulterior motives and would eventually turn against Sparta in support of the helots, dismissed the Athenian contingent. This infuriated the Athenians. They broke their alliance with Sparta and started building their own system of alliances. The rebellions were eventually put down, with the survivors fleeing to Athens, and then settling near Corinth. This location is important, as it is near the only land-bridge connecting Attica and the Peloponnesus. The Third Messenian War ended in 459 BC, and yet, more wars were soon to be fought. Wars that threatened the entire Greek way of life.

Chapter 5 – The Fight for Democracy

Although Greece was growing in many ways outside of politics, they soon faced a threat to their political system and general way of life through the war with the Persians. The wars between the Greek city-states and the Persians (technically the Achaemenid Empire), was one of the great deciding events of the ancient world; specifically, it would determine whether the region of Greece would be ruled under their favoured democracy or whether they would be taken over by an autocracy. Had Persia conquered or subjugated the Greeks, their traditions of democratic governance may have been lost forever.

Going up against the Persians was formidable. The Achaemenid Empire stretched from the Indus River valley, north into the Caucasus Mountains, the northern shores of the Black Sea, and west into Libya. At its height, the Persians controlled over two million square miles of land and had a population of between 15 and 30 million people. Before their conflict with the Greeks, the Achaemenid Empire had conquered the Neo-Babylonian Empire and the Egyptian Empire, neither of which was an easy task. Although outnumbered, the Greeks were fighting a defensive war in which they were intimately familiar with the lands and seas around them. It was with these advantages, along with Greek courage, that would eventually turn the wars in their favour.

The wars began, not in Greece-proper, but in Asia Minor, along the western coast of Anatolia; specifically, in Ionia. The cities there were populated by Greek settlers from the Ionian tribal group, and these settlers had much in common with the people in Athens. Twelve cities were founded: Miletus, Myus, Priene, Ephesus, Colophon, Lebedos, Teos, Klazomenae, Phocaea, Erythrae, the island of Samos, and the island of Chios. These cities were culturally and economically connected, but remained politically independent from one another and from the Greek mainland, until approximately 560 BC. In that year these Grecian cities were conquered by the Lydians. Sometime around 547 BC, the Achaemenid Empire conquered Lydia, and with it, these Greek cities.

Unlike in other portions of the Empire, where the Persians could find local elites to help with ruling the region, there was little help to be found in Ionia, because of their democratic and independent heritage. The Empire then decided to promote individual tyrants to rule each of the cities, which even still did not work out well.

In 499 BC, the tyrant of Miletus, Aristagoras, set sail on an expedition to conquer the island of Naxos. It was a catastrophic failure, which led Persian plans for his dismissal. Aristagoras, not wanting to be deposed, raised up the entirety of Greek Anatolia into rebellion against the Persians. This was the Ionian Revolt, which lasted until 493 BC.

The rebellion was not contained to the coastline; it drew more regions of Asia Minor into the conflict. Aristagoras, being Ionian and having cultural and religious ties to Athens, also garnered military support from Athens and nearby Eretria. In 498 BC, the combined forces of Ionia, Athens, and Eretria burned the Persian regional capital of Sardis to the ground. The Persian king, Darius the Great, boiled over in anger and vowed to have revenge on Athens, Eretria, and Ionia for this. The revolt continued until 494 BC when the Persians could mount a significant enough military and attack the city of Miletus. At the Battle of Lade, the Ionians were crushed, and the rebellion was over. The last vestiges of it were wiped out within a year.

Seeking to secure the western Asia Minor from further revolts, and from the meddling of the mainland, King Darius embarked on a plan to conquer Greece, which launched more fighting between Greece and Persia. The first Persian invasion of Greece began in 492 BC, with the Persian general Mardonius marching north through Thrace and Macedon and conquering those regions. He was stopped by a storm, which destroyed his fleet near Mount Athos, crippling his supply lines. Mardonius was then wounded in an attack by a Thracian tribe and was forced to retreat to Asia Minor.

In 490 BC, King Darius sent emissaries to all the major cities of Greece demanding their submission, or else face destruction. Most cities relented, except for Athens and Sparta, which executed the emissaries upon arrival. A second, larger force was dispatched, led by two commanders: Datis and Artaphernes. This army subjugated the Cyclades (a group of islands in the south-central Aegean). Next, the army moved against Eretria, laying siege to it for six days. The city was betrayed by two members of its ruling elite, who opened the city gate to the Persians. The army razed Eretria and enslaved those it did not kill. While marching towards Athens, the Persian force was decisively defeated at the Battle of Marathon, which put a temporary hold on Darius' ambitions.

Darius' rage burned brighter than ever, and he began to plan to completely conquer Greece. Before he could carry out his plans, he died in 486 BC. Unfortunately, his revenge-fueled rage did not die with him. His son Xerxes personally conquered Greece. In 480 BC, Xerxes led the second invasion of Greece with one of the largest ancient armies ever assembled. Historian Herodotus put the size of the Persia army at 2.5 million men. For comparison: when The Nazis invaded the Soviet Union during Operation Barbarossa they had approximately 3.8 million men. Most modern historians believe Herodotus greatly exaggerated the size of the army, instead estimating the size of the force at around 250,000 men. We cannot examine Persian accounts of the invasion because there are none; no Persian records of any of the attacks of Greece exists.

The Battle of Thermopylae consisted of just a few thousand Greeks against the Persian army (including their famous Immortals— a popular and well-renowned Persian military unit). The Greeks were betrayed by a local who showed the Persians a mountain pass through which they could flank the Greek army. Leonidas of Sparta dismissed most of the Greek army, but he remained behind with 2,000 soldiers to delay the Persian advance. The eventual Persian victory allowed them to march on Athens and set it ablaze, as well as overrun most of Attica. However, the Persians were again defeated at sea, during the Battle of Salamis, which crippled their supply lines. The next year, a united Greece went on the offensive, ultimately defeating the Persians at the Battle of Plataea, and ultimately ending the invasion of Greece.

Following the success at Plataea, the remaining portions of the Persian fleet were destroyed at the Battle of Mycale. In the North, the Persian garrisons Sestos and Byzantium were expelled, pushing the Persians back across the Bosporus (waterway located in modern-day Turkey). Due to the actions of the Spartan general, Pausanias, at Byzantium (which included releasing Persian prisoners who were his friends or relatives of King Xerxes), the anti-Persian alliance was reconstituted around Athenian leadership.

This group came to be known as the Delian League. They continued the campaign against Persia for the next 30 years. At the Battle of the Eurymedon, in Asia Minor, the Delian League won a decisive victory that secured freedom for the cities in Ionia. The League, not content with fighting Persia directly, helped also to incite a revolt in Egypt, which ended disastrously for the Egyptians and the Delian League. Following this error, further fighting against Persia was halted. The last of the fighting occurred when the Greeks sent a fleet to Cyprus in 451 BC but achieved few gains.

This series of battles came to be known as The Persian Wars. It was long, and many lives were lost, but as the Greeks won, and so did democracy. Their democratic way of life was safe once again, for at least the time being.

Chapter 6 – The Peloponnesian War

The threats of the Persian Empire had represented a threat to Greek independence, and by extension, the future of governance through democracy. Likewise, the Peloponnesian War threatened the Greek political system, by ending the polis system of governance.

In the 50 years between The Persian Wars and The Peloponnesian War, the cities of Athens and Sparta were considered 'first among equals' among the rest of the Greek city-states. However, human nature being what it is, envy, greed, and fear eventually caused a rivalry to spread. Thucydides, who was present for the conflicts and who wrote a masterful history of the period, believed the eventual war was started by Sparta. He supposed Sparta began to feel trapped by the burgeoning Athenian power. Athens and Sparta were both powerful arenas, especially after the successful conflicts against Persia. At the time, they were both run by Leagues (loose-alliances that were headed by a dominant city-state). Athens had its Delian League, and Sparta had its Peloponnesian League. Unfortunately, the two leagues were the beginning of the end for the Greek polis system.

Originally the Delian League was meant to provide the organizational structure to fight against the Persians; however, Athens began to use the League's navy for its own purposes. Further, minor city-states, in the Delian League, practiced their traditional form of democratic governance, but Athens made the major decisions. This did not sit well with the other members of the League, sparking a variety of minor conflicts. Athens had the powerful and expansive navy, along with other alliances at its disposal, which it continued to grow and develop in case Persia should return.

The Peloponnesian League was organized under more broadly democratic terms, with two council-bodies and with all the member city-states having a vote in one of the councils. Sparta held the most sway, being the only city able to call everyone together, and all the other city-states were made to have alliances with Sparta. They could also have alliances with each other, but they were not required to. Sparta also had an advantage over the other cities in that it could field a standing army of hoplite infantry (citizen soldiers), who were not bound to farmers' fields like the militaries of other city-states would have been. Also, Sparta could call up an additional two hundred thousand soldiers (Helots) from their allies and their own population.

The war between these two powerful forces began with Athens inserting itself into a conflict between Megara and Corinth, both of which were allies of Sparta. Athens was able to secure an alliance with Megara, which gave the Delian League a foothold on the Isthmus of Corinth, with which they could isolate the rest of the Peloponnesus.

Sparta was soon pulled into the conflict, which quickly widened into a greater war. This war is not what many consider the Peloponnesian War, but it functions in much the same way that World War I was the prelude to World War II. Eventually, peace would be found, but peace would be short-lived, and tempers would only smoulder.

This prelude conflict began in 459 BC, with the war between Megara and Corinth, and concluded in early 445 BC. Athens was unprepared for the conflict, and faced with a massive Spartan invasion of Attica; they were willing to accept Sparta's terms: cede lands and allies on the mainland. Both Athens and Sparta were still in control of their respective leagues and alliances. The peaceful resolution lasted only fifteen years.

The provocation that sparked the Peloponnesian War, once again, came down to Athens' relationship with Megara. In approximately 432 BC, following further problems with both Corinth and Megara (which was an ally of Sparta at this time), Athens enacted a trade embargo against the citizens of Megara. This embargo was disastrous for Megara's economy. At the request of Corinth, Sparta called together all members of the Peloponnesian League to Sparta to discuss what to do about the situation. Many of the city-states had grievances against Athens, aside from what was being done to Megara; the assembly voted, and a majority found Athens in violation of the peace. This meant war.

The Peloponnesian League, except for Corinth, were land-based powers which could field mighty armies. Just like the first conflict, Sparta and its allies invaded Attica and drove the Athenians from the countryside. Wisely, the Athens did not try and fight Sparta's vastly more superior force, and instead retreated behind its thick walls.

Furthermore, Athens still held its port and was supported by its more-than-capable navy. The Athenian leader, Pericles, had a plan: rely on the navy to ensure the increased importation of food and material into Athens, while also sending the fleet out to stabilize its coastal allies and prevent infiltrations from Sparta and its allies, all while avoiding major land engagements at any costs.

Sparta relied on a strategy of stealing crops and burning what they could not carry. While this kept their bellies full, the Spartans were unsuccessful in drawing out the Athenian army nor driving the city into capitulation. What eventually tipped the stand-off in the Spartans' favour was an outbreak of plague within the city, which killed Pericles and one-fourth of the citizens. This had given the Spartans the upper hand in the conflict.

However, even though death and disease in that battle, the Athenians were not deterred. With their refusal to surrender, both sides looked to secondary objectives throughout the Aegean, Asia Minor, and Sicily. Also, Sparta sought to turn members of the Delian League, and Athens sowed discord among the Spartan Helots.

In these subsequent conflicts, Athens used its allies' hoplites (citizen soldiers) in maritime operations, while Sparta spent time building a navy. Ultimately, during the Peloponnesian War, there were no more than a few pitched battles among vast armies. This represented a difference from how wars were fought previously, and it resulted in vast swathes of destruction, but no real change for the broader course of the conflict.

The Athenian strategy yielded some gains, primarily with the capture of Pylos in 425 BC. The Spartans, who were defending the city, were captured and there was a brief insurrection among the Helots. Not content with just capturing their enemies, Athens began to attack neutral city-states around the Aegean. This foolish decision was not the last one they made, as the Athenians also embarked on an expedition to Sicily to aid one of their allies against one of Sparta's allies. This resulted in the loss of more than 40 thousand Athenians dying in the fields of Sicily, a thousand miles away from Athens.

Sparta also established a permanent base of operations in Attica at Decelea. This was to further destabilize Athens' allies by encouraging army desertions and disrupting their economies. After the terrible plague and the disastrous foray into Sicily, Athens was unable to replace their manpower losses and soon found both their army and navy routinely outnumbered. Persia, sensing an opportunity to make inroads amongst its enemies, also subsidized Sparta, and its allies.

The Athenians finally faced defeat at a naval confrontation off Aegospotami. Sparta had won. The Long Walls, which were the lifeblood that connected Athens and its port, were burned to the ground. A Spartan force now occupied the city.

Thirty years of fighting in the Aegean, Attica, Peloponnesus, and Sicily left Athens impoverished, demoralized, and depleted. However, it was a poor outcome for both sides. Sparta and its allies were not in any position to maintain a long-term, overarching hold over all of Greece.

The Peloponnesian War had brought an end to the polis system. It had also moved armies away from the traditional way of fighting wars, where farmer-soldiers balanced their time between the battlefields and the wheat fields. Warfare now meant broad conflicts involving naval invasions, long sieges, and scorched earth approaches. Greece was wounded, and soon an invader from the North would change everything once more.

Chapter 7 – Enter Alexander the Great

North of ancient Greece proper lay the Greek kingdom of Macedon. There, Philip II ruled as king. He took a wounded Greece and attempted, through politics and force, to repair it.

In 356 BC, Philip II had a son—Alexander. His birth was marked by legendary tales. Reportedly, before her pregnancy, his mother dreamed her womb was struck by a thunderbolt. His father also dreamed he sealed her womb with a seal containing the image of a lion. Some believed Alexander's actual father was the Greek god Zeus.

It was later said that on the day of Alexander's birth, Philip's army won a battle, his horses won in the Olympic games, and the Temple of Artemis all burned. Some believed the temple burned because Artemis was not there, instead of attending Alexander's birth. Historians now believe these legends were promoted to indicate to the people of Macedon that Alexander was superhuman and destined for greatness from birth.

As a youth, Alexander was raised by a nurse and tutored. He learned to read, ride horses, hunt, and play the lire. As he moved into his teenage years, his father sought a tutor for Alexander's advanced studies. It was arranged for Aristotle to teach Alexander, along with the children of other Macedonian nobles. Many of his fellow students became Alexander's friends and later his generals. Together they learned a wide variety of topics.

Beginning at age 16, Alexander moved from the role of student to the position of regent and heir apparent for his father. He ran the kingdom while his father led troops on the battlefield. Alexander quickly responded to threats on the home-front. He colonized an area and named it Alexandroupolis. As Philip and Alexander worked together, they became increasingly involved in Greek affairs. They were a formidable team. Soon, they established a Hellenic Alliance that included most of the Greek city-states aside from Sparta. Philip was then named as the "Supreme Commander" of this new league, now called the League of Corinth by modern scholars.

Philip soon made plans to further extend his reach by attacking the Persian Empire. However, he was also distracted from his mission by love. He entered a new marriage. The relationship posed a threat to Alexander. Any children produced in the marriage could take precedence as Philip's heir. The situation started a feud between the once united father and son. Records suggest Philip even once tried to attack Alexander. Soon, Alexander fled from Macedon with his mother. He sought refuge. After a time, he learned that Philip had not intended to disown him. He returned to Macedon, but tensions continued between them, particularly over marriage arrangements.

In 336 BC, the captain of his bodyguards assassinated Philip. When Philip II died, Alexander immediately ascended to the throne. At approximately age 20, he now had charge over his own kingdom and a great army. Alexander quickly consolidated his power and further secured his reign by eliminating potential rivals. He ordered the deaths of several individuals who could have challenged his reign. Some city-states began to revolt against the reign of Alexander, but he quickly responded, using diplomacy. He soon also took on the title of "leader" (Hegemon), as Philip had.

When Alexander was given the role of generalship over Greece, he used his new position to continue extending his reach and the boundaries of his rule. He soon decided to resume his father's mission of conquering Persia. In 334 BC, he led the invasion of the Persian Empire. Records indicate he showed his intent to claim this land by throwing a spear into the soil and saying he accepted the territory as a gift from the gods.

It was the start of a series of campaigns that lasted approximately ten years. He conquered the ancient territories of Levant, Syria, Egypt,

Assyria, and Babylonia. Upon arrival at Persia, he stormed the Persian Gates. He went directly to the capital city of Persepolis, where his troops looted the city. He stayed there for five months. Then, a fire broke out in the city, which could not be stopped. Historians offer differing accounts as to Alexander's reaction to the loss. Some say he regretted it.

With little reason to stay in Persepolis, Alexander continued towards Media and Parthia. He claimed more lands, reporting the fallen leaders had named him successor to the Achaemenid throne. As he continued across Asia, Alexander established some cities bearing his name or some variation of his name. While he was leaving his mark, he also adopted elements of Persian dress and customs.

One custom that Alexander adopted was that of proskynesis, which was a show of respect to authority, comprised of a symbolic kiss on the hand or a prostration on the ground. The Greeks disliked this practice, believing Alexander intended it to deify himself. Some followers began to lose respect for him and even abandoned him. Some men conceived a plot to assassinate him. When the plot was revealed, Alexander had several people executed and killed a few himself. A next assassination attempt was exposed as well, resulting in torture and death for the would-be assassins.

As Alexander continued his conquest in Asia, he left others in charge of Macedon. He sacked Thebes to keep Greece subdued during his absence. Alexander's assigned generals kept other uprisings at bay. For the most part, while Alexander campaigned in Asia, Greece had a period of peace and prosperity. He frequently sent back sums of money and loot, which strengthened the economy of Greece. The conquests also increased the reach of trade across the entire empire.

Each victory helped to further expand Alexander's empire. Alexander's hunger for more power and dominion led him to invade India through many more campaigns and battles. Eventually, his armies became exhausted, and they refused to continue any further East. Alexander agreed to start back toward Macedon. Along the way, there was more fighting and conquering. Many men died on the arduous trek.

When he arrived in Macedon, Alexander found the leaders he had appointed had not always done as he instructed. He was disappointed in their actions and executed some. As he continued with his troops on the trek, Alexander decided to allow over-age and disabled soldiers to retire. However, they misunderstood and mutinied. They refused to be sent back home. They criticized his actions. Alexander brought in Persian leadership, and his troops soon wanted to resolve the dispute. He agreed and held a grand banquet to improve relations between his various troops. Alexander and his troops then continued their travel.

As they travelled, Alexander found more disappointing actions from the leaders he left behind. A close friend, Hephaestion, also soon died. Historians believe the death could have been the result of poisoning. Historians also believe Hephaestion could have been Alexander's lover. He was devastated by the loss and called for public mourning

Always seeking his next conquest, Alexander set out plans to invade Arabia. Alexander had the plans; however, like his father, he died before he would see them realized. On June 10 or 11 323 BC, Alexander died at age 32. His death occurred in Babylon at the palace of Nebuchadnezzar II. Historians disagree on the cause of his death. Some records suggest he got a fever that worsened until he died. Other records indicate he drank a bowl of unmixed wine and became ill, dying 11 days later. Some records suggest the death was due to poisoning. Modern historians continue to debate whether the death could have been due to poisoning or some other illness.

Alexander was interred in a gold sarcophagus filled with honey that was then placed in a gold casket. A seer had predicted that wherever Alexander was buried would see prosperity. Factions of people fought over where Alexander would be buried, with people even attempting to steal the sarcophagus. Later, the encasing was changed to glass so the gold could be used for coins. Records indicate others visited and took things from the tomb. For example, Caligula is reported to have taken Alexander's breastplate for his use. Eventually, the tomb was closed from the public. In time, the outcome for Alexander's remains and the location for his burial place were lost.

After Alexander's death, it was unclear who his heir would be. There were mixed reports for whether he had named anyone and if he had, who. Several states were ruled by his various surviving heirs and generals. Some attempted to retain order, but there were infighting and more assassinations. Claims for power and civil wars soon broke apart the empire Alexander had created. Eventually, a lack of clear leadership caused Macedonian unity to collapse. The Hellenistic world separated into these regions: Ptolemaic Egypt, Seleucid Mesopotamia and Central Asia, Attalid Anatolia, and Antigonid Macedon.

In addition to a lack of leadership, Alexander's need for more troops during his numerous conquests and campaigns had also depleted the manpower of Macedon. The divided and weakened region was unable to adequately defend itself from later attack. Ultimately, Macedon (along with Greece) became subjugated by Rome.

Despite his death and the disruption of his empire, Alexander left his mark across the world. His conquests had spread Greek culture, leaving it entwined with the customs of far-away places. This influence created a period called the Hellenistic period. Alexander settled many colonies that comprised a more magnificent Hellenistic civilization, and the influence remained years after his death.

Overall, his actions made Alexander famous as a legendary hero. In ancient times others sought to emulate him. Now, not only does his name mark approximately 20 cities such as Alexandria and Nicaea (now Punjab), but he is also featured heavily in Grecian history and myths. Further, his incredible success at military pursuits made him a measure for other military leaders to compare themselves. Therefore, his military tactics also live on long after his death.

Given his success and impact, he became known as Alexander the Great. Indeed, his influence on Greek history was significant. He is considered one of the most influential people in world history. Alexander the Great is not the only important Grecian figure to have a big effect on Greek history and leave their mark on the rest of the world.

Chapter 8 – Great Minds of Ancient Greece

While wars waged around them, some ancient Greeks chose not to become Kings or Warriors. Instead, they elected to use their minds to advance Greek culture, making discoveries, and writing works that are still relevant today.

In the world of literature and theatre, Greek poets and playwrights created significant works. One, Aeschylus, is considered "the father of tragedy," named as such because that genre mainly began with his plays. Aeschylus also changed the way plays were constructed. He wrote scripts with more characters, which allowed for more complex conflict among them. Sadly, although records indicate he wrote approximately 90 plays, only seven have survived. Even among those, some question the authorship, as to whether Aeschylus wrote them or another playwright.

Other celebrated playwrights of the time included Sophocles and Euripides. Both also wrote in the tragedy genre. Records suggest Sophocles wrote at least 120 plays, but like Aeschylus, only seven survive. His style included even more well-developed characters. Euripides likely wrote 92 plays. Like his colleagues, just some survive and among those the authorship is debated. Euripides enjoyed slightly more popularity during his time, and he also used his status to advance other theatrical innovations. For example, he started representing mythical heroes as more ordinary people. This allowed him to explore the inner life and motives of his characters. It also allowed for more romance and comedy, which expanded play genres and made the theatre more complex.

In the related world of poetry, many poets wrote great works during ancient Greece. Perhaps most famous among these was, Pindar. He was considered "by far the greatest, in virtue of his inspired magnificence, the beauty of his thoughts and figures, the rich exuberance of his language and matter, and his rolling flood of eloquence." Today, his poetry may seem peculiar to modern readers, but it was characteristic of the time.

In the world of art, artists were creating great works. Perhaps most renowned among these was Phidias. He was a painter, sculptor, and architect who advanced Classical Greek designs. Legend tells of a great statue of Zeus at Olympia that he made. It is known as one of the Seven Wonders of the Ancient World. He also made his marks at the Athenian Acropolis, with sculptures of the goddess Athena. Unfortunately, many of his great works were lost or destroyed. They have been best studied through replicas and the excavation of his workshop, which contained moulds for his bronze statues.

Greek mathematicians also had a long history of success. An early mark on the tradition was made by Euclid of Alexandria. He is considered the founder or father of geometry. He wrote a textbook, *Elements*, which was still used until the 20th century.

Archimedes was not only a mathematician, but he was also an astronomer, physicist, engineer, and inventor. Some consider him the greatest mathematician of all time. He provided many geometrical theorems, regarding the surface area, the area of a circle, and the volume of a sphere. He also offered an accurate approximation of Pi. He started applying math to phenomena in the physical world. His understanding of math allowed him to design inventions such as tools and machines.

Greek philosophy had a long history dating back to Thales of Miletus (who died in 546 BC). He may have, in fact, been the first philosopher and many regard him as the first to use a scientific philosophy. This meant he stepped away from the tradition of using mythology to explain the world and instead examined objects and phenomena through theories and hypotheses. Through this, he could recognize water was a vital substance that possibly played a role in much of nature.

The philosopher Leucippus continued to advance the study of nature during the 5th century BC. He was the first to believe everything might be composed of some invisible elements—a concept we know today as atoms. Most people are most familiar with the Greek Philosophers Aristotle, Socrates, and Plato. All three wrote on many topics and collectively their studies of philosophy significantly affected modern philosophical thought. Plato specifically founded the Academy in Athens, which was the first institution in the Western world for higher learning.

Hippocrates advanced the field of medicine in ancient Greece. His work earned him the title "father of medicine." He founded the Hippocratic School of Medicine, establishing it as a discipline and a profession. He increased medical knowledge and prescribed proper practices for the physicians of ancient Greece. So much of what he did helped to build the medical field as it is today. For example, today's doctors agree to a Hippocratic Oath, which he is credited with writing.

Finally, it is through the work of the Greek Historian, Herodotus, that so much of ancient Grecian history remains known today. He was a contemporary of other great minds such as Euripides and Socrates. He is considered "the father of history." He pioneered new ways of recording history. He would systematically investigate events and then write them into a historiographic narrative. He wrote *The Histories* to document the origins of the Greco-Persian Wars. The work had a mostly biographical tone by recounting the lives of significant figures. He also recorded the circumstances of specific battles.

Chapter 9 – Roman Take-Over

Ancient Greece was a place of almost perpetual war within the borders of Greece and the surrounding territories. Some wars meant moving boundary lines and shifts in power. A few wars resulted in a real disruption to Greek independence.

More specifically, for many years, ancient Greece was under the rule of the Roman Empire. The Roman Republic's conquering of Greece was not done in a single sweep but instead was accomplished with small and steady steps of wars and disputes over territory and power. These resulted in a slow leeching of Grecian and Macedonian autonomy. Each war and power struggle tended to be limited in scope, resulting in few territorial changes, but they were cumulative. At the end of the process, the Roman Republic came to dominate Greece and the Hellenic portions of Asia Minor and the Levant.

The downfall of Greece and Macedonia started years earlier, separate even from the influence of Rome. The challenges began after the death of Alexander the Great. At that time, his empire was divided into a handful of successor empires, each led by one of his generals. By the time of Rome's involvement, only three of those empires remained: Ptolemaic Egypt, the Kingdom of Macedonia, and the Seleucid Empire.

Ptolemaic Egypt occupied Egypt as well as small portions of what is now the Middle East and bordering Carthage to the West. The Macedonian Kingdom was the smallest of the remaining successor states, occupying only Macedonia, in northern Greece, southern Thrace, and small portions of Asia Minor. The Seleucid Empire occupied Asia Minor, the Levant, and much of modern-day Iraq. Prominent also was the rising Parthian Empire, which occupied the lands of Iran, parts of Iraq, and reached almost to the Indus River.

A war between the Roman Republic and Macedonia did not begin as a conflict between them, but instead as part of a broader catastrophic war. In 218 BC, the Roman Republic declared war on Carthage after the latter conquered the city of Saguntum (a Roman ally). The fight involved many other territories some as allies and some as adversaries. This was not the first major war between Rome and Carthage, nor would it be the last.

During the Second Punic War, after the unusually brutal and catastrophic Battle of Cannae, Philip V of Macedon felt the time was right to expand his realm at Rome's expense. To start this process, Macedonia joined the war on the side of Carthage, going against Rome with the goal of ultimately expanding their territory. However, this plan did not work, and in 214 BC Macedonia launched the First Macedonian War.

An attack on Oricum in Illyria was Macedonia's first action of the War. Rome had already been concerned that Macedonia would enter the war and cause trouble for Italy, so a single legion and small fleet were prepared for the defence. The Roman leader in charge of the legion was Marcus Valerius Laevinus. When he received word that Oricum had fallen, he easily moved the fleet and legion to recapture it. He then ordered a sub-commander to take 2,000 men to relieve the siege of Apollonia. They snuck into the city under cover of night, and in the morning rushed out of the gates and attacked the unprepared Macedonians, causing them to retreat. It was seemingly a win for Rome.

Things would soon turn against the Roman allies as Macedonia captured more Illyrian cities: Atintania, Dimale, and Lissus (the last of which gave Philip access to the Adriatic Sea). Macedonia's fleet had been destroyed or trapped elsewhere by the Romans at this point, so they had to rely on Carthage to ferry troops to the Italian peninsula.

In the Summer of 211 BC, Rome and its allies (including Greece, all in opposition to Macedonia) staged a breakout, capturing several cities and regions. Further, Rome and its allies had brokered a deal: Rome would provide the bulk of naval support and superiority, while the Greeks would conduct most of the land battles; Rome would get the slaves, and the Greeks would get the territory.

Philip V of Macedon soon found himself spread too thin, receiving requests for help from too many places and too distant for him to help: the Achaean League in the Peloponnesus, Phocis Antikyra, Aegina, and allies in Asia Minor. In 210 BC things were going so well for Rome that when Laevinus returned to Rome (to take up his consulship), he reported that the Roman legion could be withdrawn. It was determined that just the fleet would remain to provide support for the Greek allies.

In a final effort, Philip invaded southern Greece, coming into contact against Aetolians, Spartans, and Pergamene troops at the two Battles of Lamia. Both battles resulted in Macedonian victories, but at considerable costs, as the Aetolians, Spartans, and Pergamene troops merely fell back to well-fortified cities.

Five more years of hostilities continued, with both sides capturing and recapturing cities and regions. In 205 BC, the Romans re-entered the fray with over ten thousand troops, landing in Illyria. This, combined with Bithynia entering the conflict on Macedonia's side and several Greek city-states making separate peace treaties with Macedonia, meant a decisive outcome would be unlikely. A peace treaty was eventually signed, allowing Philip to have Illyria but forcing him to break his alliance with Carthage. Rome, secured now on their eastern borders and running out of allies in Greece, was satisfied. Although hostilities would erupt again during the third Punic War, which Rome again won.

War continued with the Second Macedonian War, which was significant for Greece. Like others, this war began because of a distant conflict. In Hellenic Egypt, King Ptolemy IV died in 204 BC, and his 6-year-old son Ptolemy V ascended the throne, though the realm was ruled via regents. During this transfer of power and transitional period, ancient divisions within Egyptian society spread through the country and erupted into a civil war, with Upper Egypt fighting against Lower Egypt.

Philip V (still ruling in Macedonia) and Antiochus the Great of the Seleucid Empire both looked to expand their respective realms during this period of Egyptian chaos. Philip invaded Thrace and Asia Minor; capturing Kios, Miletus, and several other independent cities. This territorial expansion worried some of the region's powers, especially the citizens and leaders in the kingdoms of Pergamon and Rhodes.

King Attalus I of Pergamon and Rhodes (territories in Greece) sent the Roman Republic a desperate plea for assistance. Rome had little interest in intervening in what they considered a strictly Greek matter. The Roman Senate did dispatch a small contingent of ambassadors to Athens to hear the Grecian concerns. Athens had recently declared war on Macedonia and Philip had responded by dispatching several thousand troops to Attica (the territory surrounding Athens).

The Roman ambassadors also met with the Macedonian general in charge of the Attica invasion force. The ambassadors delivered an ultimatum to withdraw from around Athens and leave the other Greek city-states in peace. The general of Macedonia did withdraw, but then Philip rejected the ultimatum, re-launching the invasion, and laying siege to the city of Abydus near the Dardanelles.

In 200 BC, Rome delivered a second ultimatum to the Macedonians, demanding that Philip cease his offensive attacks against all Greek cities, against any Ptolemaic cities, and enter arbitration with Rhodes and the Kingdom of Pergamon. Philip, again, rejected the ultimatum. Rome responded by landing a legion in Illyria.

The Roman intervention went terribly. The first commander, Publius Sulpicius Galba, failed as a tactical and strategic commander. His successor, Publius Villius, had to deal with a rebellion among his troops. However, Titus Quinctius Flamininus would be the commander that Rome and Greece needed. Before his appointment, the Roman ultimatum was for Macedonia to stop attacking the Greek city-states in the South; Flamininus changed it saying that Philip should abandon all Greek and Ptolemaic conquests and confine himself to Macedonia proper to allow freedom for the Greeks. This change in policy won many allies among the city-states, Flamininus was able to drive Macedonia out of Attica and back into Thessaly.

Philip asked for peace, but Flamininus was in a precarious political situation that prevented him from giving in. Roman elections were approaching, and Flamininus wanted credit for a quick war in Greece. He also did not know if he would be recalled to Rome or if his command would be extended. He decided that if he were to be recalled, he would make peace with Macedonia; however, if his command persisted, he would continue the war. After much stalling and waiting, Flamininus received good news: his command would be extended, and his allies in the Senate supported prolonging the war.

When this news reached Greece, most of Macedonia's Greek allies abandoned the war effort, and Philip was left with no other option but to hire mercenaries to continue the fight. In June of 197 BC, at the Battle of Cynoscephalae, Philip, and his mercenaries were trounced. He again asked for peace on Rome's terms. Philip eventually relinquished all conquests in Greece, Thrace, and Asia Minor. Macedonia also had to pay a war indemnity to Rome and its allies, and surrender its navy. Rome then stationed contingents of soldiers in Corinth, Chalcis, and Demetrias that did not leave until 194 BC.

When the Second Macedonian War concluded, Antiochus the Great of the Seleucid Empire sought to achieve dominion over Greece as well as Egypt. Simultaneously, Carthaginian General Hannibal Barca was advising Antiochus on military matters, and he wanted to reduce Rome to ashes. Antiochus decided to take a strategic route by manipulating a growing anti-Roman sentiment in Greece. His hope was the Greeks and Romans would fight one another, making it easier for both to be overtaken.

In 191 BC Antiochus decided to escalate again to war. He led an army across the Dardanelles. In response, Rome dispatched an army under the command of Manius Acilius Glabrio to crush Antiochus and his allies at the Battle of Thermopylae. After this crushing defeat, Antiochus found himself being chased across the Aegean Sea and back to Asia Minor. A combined Roman-Pergamon force then defeated the last army of the Seleucid Empire at the Battle of Magnesia in 190 BC. In the peace treaty, Antiochus had to pay nearly one million pounds of silver as a war indemnity, and surrender territories west of the Taurus Mountains, while Rhodes and the Kingdom of Pergamon would gain various regions in Asia Minor and Greece.

Following Philip V's death, the throne of Macedonia passed to his son, Perseus. He wanted to rebuild the kingdom, retaking the territories his father had lost, and eliminating the Roman influence in Greece. By this point, the politics of the various city-states, leagues, and kingdoms had become fractured among pro-Macedonian and pro-Roman factions. By 173 BC, Rome knew the war with Macedonia was once again on the horizon, but there was concern over who else would be dragged into the conflict. If the opponent numbers grew large, Rome's position would be threatened.

Eumenes II, King of Pergamon, made a speech in the Roman Senate in which he terrified the Senators and persuaded them that Perseus had both the means and will to invade Italy as well as to displace Rome from all of Greece. Envoys from Macedonia also spoke in front of the Senate, but it was too late, Rome was convinced Perseus had hostile intentions and that preparations for war were necessary.

The Third Macedonian War lasted for four years, and it tore apart the old alliances in Greece. At points, even Illyria and Pergamon turned against Rome. Even though the war waged for as long as it did, little ground was captured or lost for very long, due to a variety of alliances in the conflict.

There were two significant battles of consequence, Callinicus, and Pydna, that both turned the war in Rome's favour. In the first, during 171 BC, mixed armies from both sides, commanded respectively by Perseus of Macedon and Roman Consul Licinius Crassus, met at Callinicus Hill in northern Thessaly. The battle went horribly for the Romans and their Pergamon allies. They lost almost three thousand soldiers while the Macedonian-Thracian force lost less than one hundred. Perseus withdrew before the conclusion of the battle, leaving an inconclusive finish to what could have been a rout of the enemy forces.

The second decisive battle (the Battle of Pydna) occurred in the final year of the war in 168 BC. This victory allowed Rome to have its vengeance. At that battle, Rome had a new Consul, Lucius Aemilius Paullus, who did not make the tactical blunders of some of his predecessors. Even though Perseus mustered a slightly larger army (43,000 total), he lost 31 thousand of his troops, and he was taken prisoner; comparatively, for the Romans, roughly one hundred soldiers were killed. The resulting peace treaty cemented Roman hegemony over much of Greece—divided Macedonia into four smaller, pro-Roman republics, and fostered the growth of pro-Roman factions all over Greece. There was a Fourth Macedonian War, in which Andriscus of Macedon sought to re-establish the kingdom in Macedonia. This conflict was short and brutal. It resulted in the annexation of Macedonia as a province and the full assumption of Roman control over Greece. After Macedonia's defeat, the Aechaeans foolishly thought they could resist Roman control over the Peloponnesus. In response, Rome burned Corinth to the ground. With these victories and demonstrations of power, Rome was solidly in control of Greece. This began a period in which Greece was a part of the Roman Empire.

Chapter 10 – Cleopatra and her Consorts

Once Rome and the Italians had dominion over the region of Greece, it allowed for influence from a particularly well-known figure in history—Cleopatra. In fact, although Cleopatra is most associated with Egypt. She was Greek in origin.

Cleopatra was the daughter of Ptolemy XII Auletes. He ruled over Egypt for a time before being ousted. He reclaimed the Egyptian throne in 55 BC, by invading Alexandria. This made Egypt part of the Roman Empire. Toward the end of his term, Ptolemy named Cleopatra as his co-regent. When he died, he decreed she and her brother (Ptolemy XIII) should rule Egypt together. The two were married to enforce the arrangement. Then, they were both co-regents, although Cleopatra tended to rule alone.

Early in her reign, Cleopatra faced challenges as the country endured deficient floods of the Nile, famine, economic failures, and political conflicts. Simultaneously, Cleopatra further established herself as an independent ruler. Due to a poorly run conflict with the Gabiniani (powerful Roman troops stationed in Egypt to protect Roman interests), Cleopatra fell from power. Her brother was placed in charge, and she fled to exile.

However, her brother, Ptolemy, soon made a miscalculation of his own, by ordering the death of Julius Caesar's son-in-law. When Caesar arrived in Egypt, he was angry and took over as arbiter to resolve the rival claims of Ptolemy and Cleopatra. However, being cunning, Cleopatra had smuggled into the palace to meet Caesar. When the two met, they forged both a political and a romantic alliance.

Caesar helped to defeat Ptolemy's army, and so promoted Cleopatra's claim to the throne. The two soon had a son, Ptolemy

Caesar (born in 47 BC), although Caesar refused to name the child as his heir. He instead placed a grandnephew as his heir. When Cleopatra and Caesar later visited Rome, it was considered scandalous, because he was already married. After Caesar's assassination, Cleopatra returned to Egypt.

There, she ruled with her son as her co-regent. During the Roman Civil War, she sided with the Caesarian party, which was led by Mark Antony. The two soon formed a relationship. They lived in Alexandria, Egypt for a time. Cleopatra birthed twins (Alexander Helios and Cleopatra Selene II). Distance took Cleopatra and Antony away from one another for a time, but they later resumed their relationship. The two married and he soon made Alexandria his permanent home. They had one more child.

The two initially fought together against Octavian to protect Cleopatra's claims over Egypt. Later, Antony's armies deserted and joined with Octavian's. To finance her troops in the war, Cleopatra stole gold from the tomb of Alexander the Great. War is not easy, and the defeats they faced took their toll on each of them. Historians are unclear on all the facts, but it is believed they likely died by suicide (in 30 BC).

Cleopatra was the last Hellenistic ruler of Egypt. Further, because Egypt was under Roman rule at the time, her reign is also inextricably linked to the Roman Empire and back to Greece. Thus, she is a significant part of Egyptian, Roman, and Greek History.

Chapter 11 – Hadrian's Travels

Another figure most closely linked to Roman History, who by way of Roman dominion over Greece, influenced Greek history was Publius Aelius Hadrianus (Hadrian). He ruled as Roman emperor from AD 117 to 138. His rule and work were influential for the Roman Empire and Greece as its subsidiary.

Hadrian claimed to be born in Rome; however, his maternal side of the family was from Hispania (modern day Spain), and it is likely he was born outside of Italy. Hadrian's paternal lineage can be traced to an ancient town in Italy—Picenum. However, his father was also born and raised in Hispania. At age 10, Hadrian was orphaned. He was taken in as a ward of Trajan and Publius Acilius Attianus. Hadrian was educated and raised similarly to Roman aristocrats.

As a young man, Hadrian entered politics. His first post was as a judge for Rome's inheritance court. He then moved on to serve as a military tribune, under Legio II and then Legio V. In that role, Hadrian had the good fortune to inform his mentor, Trajan, he would be heir to the emperor. Hadrian served a third term as tribune for Legio XXII. His role as tribune gave him advantages for his political career.

In AD 101 Hadrian was elected to a higher public office position, that of quastor (essentially a liaison between the emperor and the senate). He continued climbing the political ranks in various positions and served on the military battlefield. Despite his successes in Rome, Hadrian decided to travel to Greece. There, he was given Athenian citizenship. He was also appointed as eponymous archon for Athens. For his work, the Greeks honoured him with a statue placed in the Theatre of Dionysus. After a time, Hadrian was called to serve Rome again. He served as a legate in an expedition against

Partha. Then, he acted as general commander of the Eastern Roman army, when Trajan became too ill to do so.

Trajan died while trying to return to Rome. Hadrian relied on close relationships with Trajan's family, especially the women of the family, to support his bid as Trajan's successor. Trajan's wife felt she and Hadrian shared the same ideals and goals for the Roman Empire, which was to run it as a commonwealth with a culture based in Hellenic customs. Unfortunately, discord between Hadrian and Trajan had somewhat derailed Hadrian's political career. Further, Trajan had stopped explicitly supporting Hadrian's political bids and did not name Hadrian as his heir. Instead, it was Trajan's wife that did name Hadrian as heir and as such many questioned the legitimacy of it. Nonetheless, the Roman Senate did support Hadrian's position.

Now, emperor, Hadrian suppressed a Jewish revolt in the east and then addressed disturbances along the Danube. While Hadrian was on the war-front, his former guardian, Attianus, ruled Rome in his stead. Attianus ordered the execution of high ranking officers because he suspected a conspiracy among them. The action, which had happened without due process, caused discord between Hadrian and the Roman Senate.

Hadrian spent much of his time as emperor outside of Italy. He appointed a close friend, Marcius Turbo, to serve when he was away. This was an unusual practice, but Hadrian wanted to see the empire. It also allowed him to make calculated moves to reshape the Empire and bring in the Hellenic culture, he so admired. Hadrian also travelled to ancient Britannia. There he ordered a wall be built separating the empire's border from this land to the North. He also visited southern Gaul and Spain. In these areas, he oversaw new constructions of temples and a basilica. He visited Mauretania, where he funded military training for young men, with the expectation they would later join the Roman military. In Euphrates, he negotiated a settlement and observed the Roman defences there. He continued along his journey and eventually arrived in Greece.

When Hadrian arrived in Greece, it was the AD 124. It was the autumn season, and he could participate in the Eleusinian Mysteries (initiations for a cult of Greek gods). While in Greece, Hadrian was active in their political life. He revised their constitution, made decisions about the economy, and created foundations to fund public games/events. He argued for the building of structures such as aqueducts and public fountains. He also helped to restore ancient shrines. All his actions served to support Roman rule over the area, by associating Roman leadership with Greek culture. He also invited Greek politicians into the Roman senate. All these actions strengthened the political connections been Greece and the broader Roman Empire.

After his activity in Greece, Hadrian set out to return to Italy. On the way, he visited Sicily. Once back in Italy, he toured the country. There, he also restored shrines and other important structures. While many appreciated his improvements, people were less accepting of his decision (in AD 127) to divide Italy into four separate regions that could be ruled by leaders (essentially like governors). Soon, Hadrian fell ill. He continued to travel. He visited Africa, and his arrival coincided with the end of a drought.

Hadrian was soon pulled back to his beloved Greece. He focused this visit on Athens and Sparta. He wanted to institute a Panhellenion council to bring all the Greek cities together in a united group. After setting that great work into motion, he continued with more travels into Egypt. There, he restored tombs and sailed on the Nile. During a trip along the Nile, Hadrian's close friend and possible lover Antinous drowned in unknown circumstances. In Antinous's honour, Hadrian established Antinopolis, an unusual temple-city complex that would run like a Greek polis.

Soon Hadrian returned to Greece, to inaugurate the Panhellenion. City-states had to show genuine Greek heritage to be a part of this. It was all part of Hadrian's attempts to protect classic Greek culture. Some at the time felt his view of Hellenistic culture was too narrow, and they were not interested in joining the Panhellenion. In contrast, others viewed Hadrian as a deity. He was given honorific titles and monuments were erected in his honour. Hadrian wintered in Athens before going east, towards Judaea.

In Judaea, Hadrian continued his works of rebuilding and improvement. Some incorrectly believed he planned to assimilate a Jewish Temple for use by the Romans. Records suggest Hadrian also intended to abolish other Jewish traditions, such as circumcision. An anti-Hellenistic and Anti-Roman uprising grew among the Jewish people. The Romans were unprepared and overwhelmed. However, they ultimately defeated the Jewish people, and it is believed they inflicted harsh punitive measures. This included removing the province from the Roman map and renaming several key areas.

Hadrian eventually returned to Rome. He was disappointed that progress towards a cosmopolitan empire had been disrupted. He continued trying to build the links between Rome and Greece, including erecting a Temple to Greek and Roman goddesses, to demonstrate the universal nature of the whole empire.

As Hadrian faced the end of his life, he had to deal with the question of who would succeed him as he had no biological children. He adopted a consul, Lucius Ceionius Commodus, to be his heir. Some suspected Lucius was Hadrian's biological son. Lucius died before Hadrian did, so Hadrian adopted Titus Aurelius Fulvus Boionius Arrius Antoninus to be his heir. This decision was not well-received.

In AD 138, Hadrian died. He was age 62. His health had been failing for some time, and it is believed heart failure may have been the cause of his death.

Hadrian had worked nearly his whole life in support of Hellenistic culture. Soon after his death another, a new threat emerged in the region, one which left destruction in its path and fear among the people of Greece and the Roman Empire. Hellenistic culture was under threat, and the Greek people were once again most focused on survival.

Chapter 12 – Gothic Raids on Greece

Although they brought destruction, leaving an enormous impact on the ancient world, the origin of the ancient Gothic (or Goth) tribes remains mostly a mystery. There is limited evidence of their travels, culture, and history before their contact with the Roman Empire, which included Greece. Archaeologists and scholars have examined multiple groups that may have comprised the Goths, hoping to discern their origins and path. However, they have reached no definitive conclusions.

The historical information becomes more clear starting in the 3rd century AD when various Gothic tribes began approaching towards Asia Minor and the Balkans. In those locations, they affected mostly Greek areas of settlement. In the beginning, these raids were limited to the northern coast of the Black Sea and the lower Danube River. This changed after the defeat of the Romans at the Battle of Arbritus in AD 251. The Battle of Arbritus was fought against a confederation of Scythian and Gothic tribesmen.

Following this victory, the Goths likely felt more confident and continued extending their reach. They began raiding and pillaging the main region of Asia Minor with impunity. Even the greatest and most ancient cities of the area could not escape their wrath. The Goths were brutal, massacring the people in their path. Entire populations were cut down to nearly nothing. This also destroyed the economic outlook for the region. Extensive Gothic raids throughout Asia Minor occurred during the reign of Emperor Valerian.

In AD 253, the Goths and their allies sought to extend their reach even further. Some Gothic groups sailed south along the coast of Asia Minor, where they reached Ephesus and Pessinus. Meanwhile, other Gothic hordes set out to raid and terrorize the Greek mainland. The Boranians (allies of the Goths), forced the Roman commander of Bosporus to give up his fleet. Next, the Gothic hordes besieged the city of Pityus, located on the north-eastern shore of the Black Sea. The city, defended by just a small Roman contingent, successfully drove off the Gothic tribesmen.

Not willing to give into defeat, approximately one year later, the Goths returned to once again claim that region. They were more successful on their second attempt, and the city of Pityus fell to them. Following this success, they sailed south towards Trebizond— a city defended by thick walls and a Roman garrison. The Romans were not adequately prepared. Some Boranians managed to climb the walls of Trebizond and open the gates to the others. After looting the city and enslaving any surviving people, the Goths and Boranians triumphantly set sail towards home, returning across the Danube.

A second Gothic campaign against Greece and Asia Minor occurred in approximately AD 257. The Goths, confident they could repeat their successes, sailed with a large fleet towards the northern coasts of Asia Minor. Their army followed on land and sea, carving a path of destruction along the western coast of the Black Sea. This time, their primary target was the city of Bithynia but this did not stop them from wreaking havoc along their entire path. The garrison defending the city of Chalcedon abandoned their posts, leaving the city undefended. It was easily conquered. The Goths followed this destruction with some more, by burning down the city of Nikomedeia, which was also abandoned by its defenders. They then continued their path, raiding each city they arrived at. Emperor Valerian could do nothing to stop the rampaging Goths and their allies. The destruction only ceased when the Goths finally tired, deciding to return home.

Seeking a third campaign of death and destruction, the Gothic hordes set out again in approximately AD 260. Additionally, other Germanic tribes established their place in the region. This additional threat contributed to the already present chaos. In about AD 268, the

Goths felt pressured to settle down on the south shore of the Dniester River. They arrived with a large army and fleet, including Gothic allies. The military was the largest unified force to invade the Roman Empire during the 3rd century. The army and navy rampaged throughout the region, inflicting their usual destruction.

More recently, historians have discovered portions of an ancient Greek text that describes the influence the Goths inflicted on Greece specifically. The Goths began a raid on Greece by attempting to attack the Grecian city of Thessalonica. The Greeks there successfully defended themselves. The Goth force turned southward toward Athens. The text describes a battle fought at Thermopylae in a narrow pass there, where the Goths were blocked from advancing. They were inspired to stand strong against the Goths with whatever weapons they might have available to them. The outcome of this battle stand-off is not known as the historical records are incomplete.

The psychological impact of frequent Gothic raids was enormous. This was true even for people living further inland, who were less at risk of attack because it was rarely a target for the Goths, as they tended to stay near waterways. Everyone lived in sheer terror of the distant threat. For example, the residents of Stratonikeia made invocations to Zeus at his temple in Panamara, asking if the city would be attacked. Legend says Zeus communicated they would not allow their city to fall into the hands of the barbarians.

The panic felt by many residents of the region was magnified by the fact the Roman garrisons could rarely stop the Goths. Several times, the garrisons just abandoned their posts or cities, and the residents were left unprotected. This, combined with the Gothic threat, left people terrified they would be attacked and enslaved.

In AD 268, the penultimate battle between the Goths and Romans took place in Naissus of Upper Mysia. The Goths, who were frequently away for months at a time, were also having difficulty getting more provisions. Although they received reinforcements from beyond the Danube, they were finally defeated in 269. The

Romans killed or captured 50,000 barbarians and set many of the captured to work as slaves on farms in the region. Although smaller in scale, new waves of barbarians, including Goths attempted to attack again, but they were driven back by approximately AD 277.

In AD 297, the eastern regions of the Roman Empire, nearby and including Greece received more reinforcements to protect against future invasions. Various emperors also worked to redefine the political relations with the Goths, offering peace and keeping them at bay. The hope was to keep this threat in check. These political moves created a peaceful relationship that lasted until the reign of Constantine.

These agreements did not entirely stop all raids, and there was still the occasional attack from some Gothic horde. However, the days of Gothic terror were now behind the people of Greece and the broader Roman Empire. Meanwhile, another dominant force had started to move into the region which would create extensive change.

Chapter 13 – Rise of Christianity

History moves in tandem. Even while wars were fought, and power shifted among hands, another influential movement was spreading through Greece (and the Mediterranean as a whole). That movement was Christianity, and it would strongly influence Greek history.

It is notable that in the first century AD, approximately three-quarters of the Christians, within the Roman Empire, spoke Greek. The scriptures the Christians read were in Greek. Many Christians, before the journeys of Paul, were former adherents of the Jewish faith, and their scriptures were in Greek. Later books of the Bible were originally written in Greek and used expressions, idioms, and illustrations that were easily understood by the Grecians or others familiar with Greek culture. However, neither Jesus nor the apostles nor any of the writers of the New Testament were Greeks. They were all Jewish.

One might wonder how the Greek language becomes so crucial in the spread of Christianity. One might also wonder how those earliest Christian writers, missionaries, and apologists came to present their message, so it was easily understood by Greek-speaking people. Scholars offer answers to these questions through the lens of history.

Under Roman rule, especially during and after the rule of Hadrian, the major cities of Asia Minor, Syria, and Egypt still flourished as centres of Greek culture. This Greek culture acted like glue, binding the people in the eastern realms of the Empire. Hellenism acted upon every part of life, including institutions of government, law, commerce, trade, industry, and even fashion. Typically, Athenian design influenced the development of most Greek cities, and there were structures that would have been found in Athens during its primacy: gymnasiums, theatres, public forums, and temples. Ancient

Greece was initially polytheistic, but this changed as Christian missionaries arrived.

The history of Christianity expands far past the boundaries of Greece itself. Just as the Greek language influenced the spread of Christianity, the spread of Christianity affected the course of Greek history (alongside other regions of the Mediterranean).

Among the earliest Christian missionaries to preach in the Greek world, no one was more prominent than Paul. To this day, visitors to Athens can stop at the base of the Areopagus and inspect a bronze plaque commemorating Paul's famous speech there. The account is recorded in the seventeenth chapter of the Book of Acts. The opening words, "Men of Athens," were standard for a Greek orator and were intended to ingratiate himself to his audience, primarily Epicurean, Stoic, and other philosophers.

Instead of criticizing their faith, Paul acknowledged the long tradition of Greek polytheism. This polytheism, by the time Paul arrived, had become so complex in its structure, the people had concluded they might have missed an important deity in their worship. Therefore, they had even erected an alter "To an Unknown God." Paul capitalized on this belief and went on to describe this "Unknown God" as the God known within the Christian faith. According to the account written in Acts, after his preaching, some important figures believed in these new teachings and followed Paul's offering of Christianity: Dionysius the Areopagite, Damaris, and others.

In this way, Paul had reached his listeners by using concepts they could understand. The Stoics at the time agreed with him that God is the source of human life, that all men belong to the same race, that God is not far off from common man, and that human life is dependent on God. Paul supported this last point by citing works of the Stoic poets, Aratus and Cleanthes. Epicureans also found points in common with Paul—that God is alive and can be known, is self-sufficient, requires nothing from men, and does not dwell in handmade temples. These points of the agreement helped many at the time accept Christianity.

However, not all who heard of Paul's work were accepting of it. After years of preaching and missionary work, Paul was persecuted, arrested, tried, and executed in Rome during the reign of Emperor Nero. Further Christian persecution occurred intermittently over the following two centuries, starting with approximately the Great Fire of Rome in AD 64 under Nero. The persecution of Christians in the Roman Empire was carried out by the state and local authorities. Beginning in AD 250, empire-wide persecution took place by decree of Emperor Decius. The decree was in force for 18 months, during which time some Christians were killed while others apostatized to escape execution.

Christians finally saw a reprieve from their centuries-long persecution, under Emperor Flavius Valerius Constantinus (also known as Constantine I or Constantine the Great). Contrary to his predecessors, Constantine saw value in the growth of Christianity. Once he became the sole Emperor (there was a tetrarchy when he first came to power), he took steps to remove all the legal restrictions on Christianity and brought an end to any official, state-sponsored, persecution.

In the Edict of Milan, composed in AD 313, Constantine offered citizens of the Empire new freedoms and protections from centuries-old bigoted edicts. No doubt, fourth–century Christians felt peace like none before as they read (or heard) of the Edict of Milan. Constantine's conversion to Christianity is controversial and still debated by historians. Scholars are not sure if it was done for personal or political reasons.

However, even before becoming the sole emperor, Constantine had spoken of a dream that he had before a pivotal battle with Maxentius at the Milvian Bridge (AD 312). In the dream, God told Constantine to have the Christian "Chi-Rho" monogram painted on his soldiers' shields to ensure success. Whether it was due to desperation or blind faith, he submitted to the instructions of his dream, carried a new banner of allegiance into battle, and won the battle, even against a troop size double twice his size.

With his victory achieved, and with the drowning of Maxentius earlier in battle, Constantine went on to become sole emperor of an undivided empire, which allowed him to become a victor for Christianity as well. In fact, his actions paved the way for Christianity to lead society rather than be persecuted.

By the 5th century, Christianity was the state religion of the Roman Empire, including Greece. This lead to massive changes in how the faith functioned within society. Because the era of persecution was over, there was a move from private to public worship. Christianity also became a community affair, especially once theological debates and heresies began to surface. Christianity also changed its organizational structure, going from a very localized, congregation-focused set of operations to a formal, stratified structure with differing levels of authority. Additionally, Christian leaders could decide how Christianity would fit in with law and governance, deal with barbarian peoples, and handle the sort of problems that come with any developed society.

Constantine's rule was the dawn of a new era in the Roman Empire. He built a new imperial residence at Byzantium and renamed the city, Constantinople, after himself. It became the capital of the Empire for more than one-thousand years. After more border and cultural changes, the region was eventually called the Byzantine Empire. That change coincided with the close of ancient Greek history and the beginning of the Medieval Period.

Chapter 14 – End of Antiquity

Although Christianity was rising in the region, the hold of Roman rule was starting to decline, leading eventually to a total change in the Grecian way of life. That change resulted in the turn-over from Roman Rule to Greece becoming a part of the Byzantine Empire. The progressing changes in rule and culture also led to events constituting the end of antiquity because it spurred the region to move out of the period of ancient Greece. However, like anything, it took many steps and events to get there.

From the time of Emperor Diocletian, who ruled in multiple roles as either sole emperor, co-emperor, or part of a Tetrarchy, from AD 284 to 305; the Roman Empire went through serious and long-lasting changes. The Empire was also on a declining trajectory. Several Diocletian's efforts both pushed back against and accelerated, this decline. For example, the tetrarchy divided the Empire to simplify administration and governance. However this division tended to confuse the border regions, and caused further complications when one tetrarch would die before the others.

Although Constantine managed to rule over a unified Roman Empire until his death in AD 337, this unity proved illusory and could not be sustained. In AD 364, Emperor Valentinian I again divided the empire into western and eastern sections, putting himself in power over the west. He appointed his brother Valens to rule over the east. The fate of the two regions diverged considerably over the next several centuries.

In AD 451 the Council of Chalcedon officially established the Christian world into five distinct patriarchates, each ruled by a Patriarch: Rome, Alexandria, Antioch, Jerusalem, and Constantinople. In AD 476, the barbarian Odoacer overthrew the last

Roman emperor (Romulus Augustus) captured Rome, and made himself King of Italy.

Then, in the late 4th century, the migration of Germanic tribes also further disrupted the Empire, eventually resulting in the total collapse of the Western regions. Those places were then replaced by something considered the Barbarian Kingdoms. This meant a decline in the prominence of Grecian culture. Soon, in fact, the Greco-Roman, Christian, and Germanic groups were intermixing, including fusing their cultures together. This laid the foundations for a new developing culture in Western Europe.

Meanwhile, the Eastern half of the Empire benefited from a strong administrative core and political stability, as well as significant wealth compared with other states. The Eastern emperors were also able to exert and maintain control over the empire's economic and military resources to muster sufficient manpower if a hostile force should invade. These advantages provided the Eastern Roman Empire (known then as the Byzantine Empire or Byzantium) the ability to out-survive the Western Roman Empire by almost one thousand years. It also helped maintain Greek culture and language in those regions.

In AD 527, Justinian I became Emperor and reigned until his death in AD 565. Justinian was the first, truly Byzantine Emperor. During the years of his reign, he endeavoured to regain the lands to the West that had been lost to barbarian forces and re-establish the great empire again. His armies were led by the capable and charismatic General Belisarius, who did successfully re-conquer portions of the former Western Roman Empire, including North Africa. Justinian helped grow the empire in other ways too. Many great monuments of the Empire were also built during his reign, including the domed Church of Holy Wisdom, or Hagia Sophia, which still stands today. Justinian also reformed, simplified, and codified Roman law, establishing a Byzantine legal code that lasted for centuries and helped to shape the modern concept of the state and governance.

At the time of Justinian's death, the Byzantine Empire was the largest and most influential state in Europe. However, this came at a steep price. Debt began to mount during his various campaigns and conquests. It produced a severe strain on imperial finances. To accommodate for this, both Justinian and his successors levied a series of massive taxes on Byzantine citizens. Furthermore, the imperial army reduced in size. The army eventually became too dispersed to maintain control over the Empire's now larger borders. A new, even more dangerous threat arose in the form of Islam. In AD 634, Muslim armies began their assault on the Byzantine Empire by storming into Syria. By the end of the century, Byzantium lost Syria, the Holy Land, Egypt, and North Africa to Islamic forces.

Scholars are hard-pressed to name one date or even year to mark the end of the Antiquity in Greece. Some wars and losses marked changes in the region. However, there were slower changes in culture. Greece had been its own dominant culture. It had been influenced by Roman culture. It had been a new mix of cultural attributes within the Byzantine Empire. Over the years after the Muslim invasions, the culture of Greece continued to change. Aspects were lost, others evolved, and new attributes developed. Ultimately, the gradual socioeconomic changes between ancient and medieval Greece cannot truly be marked by any one date. Despite all the changes, the legacies of ancient Greece have lived on, influencing future generations and far off places.

Conclusion

Given its historical roots and influence on culture, Greece is now considered the "cradle of Western civilization." It birthed democracy and philosophy. It advanced literature and mathematics. Great figures left their mark on history and remain a part of our modern culture, even in entertainment through books and movies. The significant sites of ancient Greece remain, and visitors travel there to see the architecture and art.

Even after the ancient times, Greece continued to undergo changes that influenced the rest of the world. This included being under the Ottoman Empire for a time. The Greek Orthodox Church also developed and influenced modern Greece, along with the religious landscape in the rest of the world. Modern Greece continues to practice democracy, and the people there enjoy a good economy, quality of life, and positive standard of living.

Today, Greece (officially known as the Hellenic Republic) remains as a country located in Southern Europe with its capital in Athens. The borders of today's Greece place it on the southern edge of the Balkan Peninsula. Its borders meet Albania to the northwest, Turkey to the northeast. Toward the North lie the Republic of Macedonia and Bulgaria. The lower part of the country is surrounded by seas as it has the longest coastline among countries in the Mediterranean. The country is marked by mountains and surrounding islands. It is divided into nine geographic regions, including Central Greece, Macedonia, Peloponnese, Thessaly, Epirus, Thrace, Crete, the Ionian and the Aegean Islands. After years of wars and conflict, the country now mostly enjoys peace and prosperity.

Sources for Reference

The Hellenistic World from Alexander to the Roman Conquest: A Selection of Ancient Sources in Translation by Michael M. Austin

The World of Late Antiquity: AD 150-750 by Peter Brown

Readings in Ancient Greek Philosophy: From Thales to Aristotle By S. Marc Cohen, Patricia Curd, and C. D. C. Reeve (Editors)

Hadrian and the Triumph of Rome by Anthony Everitt

A War Like No Other: How the Athenians and Spartans Fought the Peloponnesian War by Victor Davis Hanson

Ancient Greece: From Prehistoric to Hellenistic Times by Thomas R. Martin

Roman Conquests: Macedonia and Greece by Philip Matyszak

A Short History of Byzantium by John Julius Norwich

A Companion to Ancient Macedonia By Joseph Roisman and Ian Worthington (Editors)

Hellenic Religion and Christianization C. 370-529 by Frank R. Trombley

Encyclopedia of Ancient Greece By Nigel Wilson (Editor)

ABOUT CAPTIVATING HISTORY

A lot of history books just contain dry facts that will eventually bore the reader. That's why Captivating History was created. Now you can enjoy history books that will mesmerize you. But be careful though, hours can fly by, and before you know it; you're up reading way past bedtime.

Get your first history book for free here:
http://www.captivatinghistory.com/ebook

Make sure to follow us on Twitter: @CaptivHistory
and Facebook: www.facebook.com/captivatinghistory so you can get all of our updates!

CPSIA information can be obtained
at www.ICGtesting.com
Printed in the USA
BVHW051432250122
627119BV00004B/378

9 781647 484897